Half Lives

TUESDAY JULY 26ᵀᴴ
1, 2, 3, 9, 13, 17, 38, 39

THURSDAY JULY 28ᵀᴴ
43, 60, 61, 62, 63

Half Lives

PETRARCHAN
POEMS

Richard Jackson

Autumn House
Press

"Autumn House" and "Autumn House Press" are registered trademarks owned by Autumn House Press, a non-profit corporation whose mission is the publication and promotion of poetry.

Text and cover design: Kathy Boykowycz
Cover painting: Metka Krašovec

Autumn House Press
Executive Director: Michael Simms
Director of Development: Susan Hutton
Community Outreach Director: Michael Wurster
Assistant Editor: Jack Wolford
Editorial Consultant: Eva Simms
Media Consultant: Jan Beatty

Printed in the U.S.A. by Thomson-Shore of Dexter, Michigan
All Autumn House books are printed on acid-free paper and meet the international standards for permanent books intended for purchase by libraries.

ISBN: 1-932870-00-8 (trade paper)
ISBN: 1-932870-01-6 (trade cloth)
Library of Congress Control Number: 2004106227

for Terri
and for Amy

Ama chi t'ama
—Petrarca, CV
Emily, Anna

In memory of Bill Matthews who
encouraged these poems from the
beginning.

Special thanks to Jerry Stern and
Stanley Plumly who have been so
supportive of this project.

By Richard Jackson

POETRY
Part of the Story (Grove Press, 1983)
Worlds Apart (Alabama, 1987, 1989)
Alive All Day (Cleveland State, 1992, 2000)
Heart's Bridge (Aureole, 1998)
Heartwall (Massachusetts, 2000)
Svetovi Narazen: Selected Poems (Ljubljana, Slovenia, 2001)
Unauthorized Autobiography: New and Selected Poems (Ashland, 2003)

CRITICISM
Acts of Mind: Interviews with Contemporary American Poets
  (Alabama 1983, 1987, 1989)
Dismantling Time in Contemporary American Poetry (Alabama, 1987)

CHAPBOOKS
The Woman in The Land: Pavese's Last Poems (Black Dirt, 1989)
Richard Jackson: Greatest Hits (Pudding House, forthcoming)

Introductory Note

These poems are loosely based on some of Petrarch's Canzoniere; they are not translations or imitations, but rather should be thought of as a kind of far ranging jazz riff off a standard tune, the way Coltrane reinvents "Bye Bye Blackbird" on his Swedish tour, changing harmonics, building from fragments. I envisioned Petrarch alive today, writing to free himself of Petrarchanisms, but keeping his rhymes. I also had in mind the adaptations of Wyatt, Surrey and Sydney, often wildly different take-offs of the same poems by Petrarch, yet these are often more personal than my other poems.

Acknowledgments

Some of these poems, sometimes in earlier versions, appeared in:
Shenandoah, Jubilat, Slope, Third Coast, Green Mountains Review, Passages North, Louisville Review, Hayden's Ferry, Southern Indiana Review, Maryland Poetry Review, Nebraska Review, Onset Review, Pembroke Magazine, The Lyric, Cafe Review, Lit Rag, on line at *Literary Potpourri, Drexel Online Journal, Hotel Amerika* and *Verse Daily,* and in two chapbooks, *Heart's Bridge* (Aureole, 1999) and *The Half Life of Dreams* (Black Dirt, 1997). Several poems also appeared in *Unauthorized Autobiography* (Ashland, 2003).

Contents

1 The Apology

2 The Battle

3 Desire's Escape

4 The Pilgrim

5 The Prodigal

6 The Dreams

7 Desire's Departure

8 To His Words

9 The Prison

10 The Prayer

11 The Promises

12 The Declarations

13 The Poet's Death

14 The Window

15 The Actor

16 Love's Apology

17 The Rumor

18 The Answer

19 The Poetics of Love

20 The Quandary

21 The Betrayal

22 Love's Contraries

23 Loyalty

24	The Turns
25	The Ruins
26	Belief
27	The Waking
28	Morning Song
29	The Cave
30	The Path
31	The Conspiracy
32	The Pause
33	The Collapse
34	The Hunt
35	The Trailhead
36	The Sparrow
37	The Exile
38	The Kiss
39	Her Soul
40	The New Style
41	The Fear
42	The Solitary
43	Her Death
44	The Surrender
45	The Solution
46	The Loss of Breath

47	Inspiration
48	The Debt
49	The Valley
50	The Plea
51	Love's Inferno
52	The Birds
53	The Loss of Myth
54	The Nightingale's Lament
55	The Trial
56	The Legacy
57	Not Here
58	The Messengers
59	To Death
60	The Model
61	The Spirit
62	The Mask
63	The Confession
65	Epilogue: Love's Myths
73	Sources

THE AUTUMN HOUSE POETRY SERIES

Michael Simms, editor

OneOnOne by Jack Myers

Snow White Horses, Selected Poems 1973-1988 by Ed Ochester

The Leaving, New and Selected Poems by Sue Ellen Thompson

Dirt by Jo McDougall

Fire in the Orchard by Gary Margolis

Just Once, New and Previous Poems by Samuel Hazo

The White Calf Kicks by Deborah Slicer
    (2003 Autumn House Poetry Prize, selected by Naomi Shihab Nye)

The Divine Salt by Peter Blair

The Dark Takes Aim by Julie Suk

Satisfied with Havoc by Jo McDougall

Half Lives: Petrarchan Poems by Richard Jackson

*The Apology
↳ a "defense" in Classical Literature

Whoever hears in these scattered rhymes the raw sighs → he believed it back then
my heart devoured when I was younger, or sees the soul's
tattered phrases hanging there unclaimed, don't scold
this art written by my other self, filled with confusion, not lies,
and forgive even this varied style I use now, that flies
as darkly as the crow, that scans the secret life of the mole,
that covers itself in Hope's blankets, that has always told
Love's truth, that now asks for pardon before its words run dry.
I know how rumor grew like a moth from a cocoon,   → nice!.
how some of you laughed when Shame stood at my door
for years, how Regret tracked me with her silent screams—
but also, and how each tree bears some fruit, how the moon
and the stars, the wind, the whole earth are images whose doors
open other worlds, if they only endure like the half life of dreams. → hmm...
                                    ↳ book title allusion...

       ✱ poets apology to reader For not allowing a better understanding
                                    ∧ Levin

conceit → extended metaphor in poetry

✳ *The Battle*

It started with simple personification: Love, waiting around in feeling's forest,
hunched ragged over low fires, wanted to punish me for my thousand slights,
and that same Love patiently picked the right time and place to strike
with its taut bow— yes— just like you read about in Ovid and all the rest.
Or, you could also say that my practiced Virtue, and you've guessed
there wasn't a lot to begin with, fleeing for cover to my armor-plated Heart,
couldn't hold off the frontal attack Love made, was blown apart,
overrun, you pick the metaphor— placed under a sort of house arrest.
Or that my Mind, harassed but not surrendering to these early assaults,
not willing to retreat when its strength, its arms, its space ran out,
fought on— though, I admit, the Heart always wanted to surrender—
then retreated to a hill, a castle of right thinking, high and difficult,
trying to withdraw gracefully from destruction, from what becomes a rout
by Slander, by Disgrace— God, against such a foe we don't have any power.

Desire's Escape

When Desire turns mad, crazed with following her
who has gnawed a terrible way out of Love's snares,
through brambles and bogs, like some deserting legionnaire,
then they both abandon me to the cliffs and weather-beaten firs;
and when I try to call Desire back to my path, he prefers
to defy Reason's maps, to forget the safest ways, to dare
the Heart's white water rapids, the sudden waterfalls of Despair,
beyond any poem's control, no matter how often I put him to the spur—
and when this Desire takes the bit himself, seeing an open meadow
he thinks will give him an edge on Love, he drags me behind
as he moves with shadows across the grass towards Love's death—
until we come to her tree planted out of love long ago,
and gather Memory's fruit, a poison that makes us blind
with Hope and fear, a nectar that brings a suffocating breath.

[handwritten marginalia: "interesting concept", "hmm...", "why not capitalized", "why no CAPS?"]

3

The Pilgrim

Take the example of that twisted, white-haired beggar, Desire—
he leaves not only the sweet home of his mind, but the family,
his real life, and they watch him pack, unable to see what he sees,
and they huddle like conspirators as he shuts the wooden door,
as he drags the withered life he's made for himself across the years,
begging a little from this hour, a little from that minute, as he flees
one Greed he hitches a ride with, even believes a second Greed,
a second Self, who robs him of his name and rips his fears
up like letters from home, and he stumbles, following this tattered dream,
into Rome to gaze and pray at the wooden or marble likeness of his savior
who could be anyone by now, he's that desperate, any hope left for a future—
this is the way, this true example, this beggar's life, the heart's debris
scattered about, this is the way I follow your name, follow your
image, never to touch what is real, though my hope, like his, endures.

The Prodigal

As the fisherman, nets ripped, his catch abandoned to the sea,
the weight of storm clouds weighting him down like his anchor,
his crew's faces pale as yesterday's fish floating in the harbor,
happy to be in port, gives thanks, falling to his knees;
or as the innocent man who feels the rope's fiber suddenly
loosened, himself freed, walks a street he dreamt of hours before—
as happy as these I am to see you have put up your sword,
my friend, stopping your war on Love. So, listen to my decree:
anyone who praises love in life or poetry or art,
welcome back that prodigal weaver of images and visions,
honor him, that prodigal lover, as if he were your own self,
and know our lives as tapestries made from the heart's
fibers, that we may stray after false images and words, but return,
like him, like me; only in Love's poverty do we value love's wealth.

The Dreams

Each day is the deer that flees into the shadows,
that seems so fragile it never occurred, never began.
Each day a few cloudless hours begin to tow
the past across the sky's memory. The heart scans
the world to find a stable soul to build upon.
How blind the stars were, how blind the moon to hope
anything would remain. Already she has gone,
already my heart seems hung by death's rope—
until I see her soul wherever I look for her
in trees, clouds, stars, the moon, my own
heart walking the streets, more in love forever
by dreaming where she is, what she is doing, what town
her voice visits, what words she uses to cover
our past — the heart's despair, the wind's frown.

Desire's Departure

When the fire dampens a fire, when the rain dries up
a river, when the wind settles tonight's tropical storm,
when Desire conquers desire, then every likeness will swarm
to Love's hive, and sometimes even opposites will hide
within opposites. My single soul, then, this disguise
I wear in the shape of my love's heart, this worn
Hope that shrinks and withers before it is really born,
only dies as love grows, and grows as love dies.
Maybe, as the waterfall deafens us where we stand,
as the sun blinds anyone who observes it too intently,
as the wind pokes among the ashes for a glowing coal,
maybe my Desire which I wear and display like a brand,
maybe this Desire is the sky itself that seems so finally
empty—and so maybe my leaving will make your leaving slow.

To His Words

I'm fed up with guarding the vague borders
your meanings desert for lies, my ungrateful words,
and still you begin your campaigns to try to purge
all emotion from my love, bringing me shame and surrender;
the more I send messengers to regain my honor
the more your envoys seem detained, or lured
to some greater meanings, or have their senses blurred,
letters stolen, visions lost in the labyrinths of some dreamer.
My tears can't hear commands to make them halt,
but march on, picking up stray syllables along the way
or hiding in the roadside bushes in times of peace—
and these famous sighs, they mope around the tents, play
cards or dice with the malcontents always ready to find fault—
Only my eyes have phrases the heart can read and seize.

✳ The Prison

If, counting these crumpled hours where the blind torturer,
Desire, has stretched each Hope on the rack or strapped
each dream to the stake, if I haven't been altogether deceived,
now, while I speak, the hour promised to me and Mercy flutters
away like a bird escaping the hunter. What shadow smothers a seed
from the sun, like this Love does, as it was about to become the desired
fruit? What beast roars in the sheepfold of my soul? Whose voice is mired
like a cart in the mud? Why is the word's grain kept from the market forever?
And here— why would Love bring me to this dungeon and disappear?
Why would Hope confess to Love what it only falsely dreamt?
Why has Sorrow abandoned any hope of ever breaking free?
I may never know, except to remember what someone wrote somewhere
on these walls: that before his death, before the soul finally wept
for its last escape, there could be no day that was not agony.

The Prayer

Blessed be the year climbing its cliffs, the month crossing the fields
of hours and days, the bridges of minutes, the grass where we stood
that first moment, the festival music keeping our time, the hood
of the season's sky above us, the moment's fictive shield
against history, her tattered glance, her broken smile, everything real
or imagined, bless the rivers I invented to carry us, the woods
I planted as our own, bless even the sweet hurt, even the herd
of stars that trample my real heart which she has taught to heal.
Blessed be these trackless words running downstream
following the remote valleys she has cut through my life,
and blessed be the sounds they cannot make, but mean,
and blessed be all these pages watermarked with her name,
these thoughts that wander the unmapped roads of strife
and love, her blessed world whose dream is always a dream.

The Promises

Trust, dressed in her most luxurious gown, led me,
with alluring promises, to open the door to my former prison,
then locked me in her damp, stony days within the walls of Reason,
giving the keys to Love, the Heart's conspirator, my recent enemy.
Disguised and held even from my former self, I tried
sending out messages coded behind these words, burned
kindling cut from my best dreams, my most secret plans,
until—who'd believe it, the doors opened from this sty—
and now like a prisoner branded with a fated number,
I carry this history, these broken chains, and my heart
seems tacked, like a poster on the gates, to my brow and eyes.
When you find my soul burrowed under this flesh, you'll remember
how I used to walk these streets, and then, frightened to a start,
ask: who lives this much that even in death can't die?

The Declarations

I have always loved, I have loved more strongly than the rope of time
that knots one day to another, loved the way the last darkness embraces
the dawn, and I shall always love this sweet and brambled place
where I return tearfully each time Love stumbles, each time
I remember how we first met here, and I will always love the time
it seemed that the sky not only reflected but *was* your face,
always love the hour that opened like a path before me into a space
where your name seemed blazed on every tree, every casual rhyme.
I have loved, this conflicted way, every messenger minute, every prodigal place,
and now they force the door of my heart just when I remember what is real—
for I had forgotten how your leaving made a desert of all time.
Still, I have loved even this: that I can feel how Hope keeps pace
with Desire, can feel each dream, each bit of life I can steal
from Love's pockets, even as it turns, sentencing me for this crime.

The Poet's Death

(William Matthews)

Cry, and let Love join in with his horn, his music sliding
down the scales to depths that call to us, pitiful lovers,
in every melody and land, for that poet who forever
honored us has died, and all the stars stop shining.
I pray that this sorrow which freezes the birds on wing,
which scorches the seas and puts the galaxy in a fever,
will not scour our weaker hearts of love forever—
because a loss this deep seems to put an end to everything.
Let Poetry also cry, then, with every image and verse,
for that master of Love and wit who could make a tree seem wise,
allow the day to begin, and make two bleak notes a harmony—
Let the city cry too, for there wasn't a soul more generous,
more forgiving, so that even the stars have tried to apologize
for not sweeping away his darkness, as he does now, in memory.

The Window

In front of each wall she makes from the heart's window,
wherever she makes the midnight bloom with light,
before each window that leads beyond the earth's shadow
towards stars and winds and ages beyond our sight—
or here, on some granite cliff where she throws
my name and all my past from its lonely height—
or the stones she walked, transformed by her shadow
into some invisible road the planets follow through the sky—
or in that place where I first saw her by a lake
in the Alps, a pass where Spring itself grazes and winters—
until, as now, each pain, each loss begins to wake—
then everything returns, everything blooms as it withers,
my heart declines, but knows it can't begin to remake
itself, — here, where even a tear could shed a tear.

The Actor

Caesar, when Ptolemy, that Egyptian traitor,
gave him the gift of noble Pompey's head,
kept his joy in the closet of his heart, so it's often said
by scholars, and wept up a storm in his eyes with tears.
And Hannibal, orphaned like a slave by his empire
and by its Fortune broke as a beggar, eating bread
on doorstoops, laughed loudly through the alleys instead
of aiming the bitter spears of his disdain through his tears.
And so, you see, this is how the soul plays its role,
its face clearly showing what it does not feel,
cloaking its passions in shadows, in words that roll
like gems from the merchant's tray, that steal
their strength from dark corners—and why all I told
you is a way to hide my anguished tears, a way to heal.

Love's Apology

Dear friend, let me apologize for the ache of flowers in the sun,
for the way my heart has wandered with the sterile bee,
for the avalanche of cold looks others gave you for knowing me,
because the shadow of this voice has torn our lives asunder
now with the tangled ropes and paths of desire for her,
now with her anchorless moon of pure disdain from me,
now with my desire clothed in rags of anguish over her,
now with her lighthearted drowning of my words in mockery's sea.
With the secrets the tree holds about the wind, she sang:
with a dream that could touch the face of the sky she stepped;
with a tattered map of her life I followed my unknown, uncertain life;
with her touch of absence, with her fog of glances, hopes prolonged,
with her pile of shadows, I'll always live, dear friend. Please accept
this apology for that storm of tongues demolishing this boarded up life.

❧ The Rumor

Those rhymes of yours full of pity for me, whose feeling
and care could bend the sky and twist the line of sight,
whose affection seems unmatched, to you I write,
if only to let you know I'm still here, still living!
No, I haven't been consumed yet by that wolf's fangs,
the very animal I adore and wait upon. Listen, in spite
of warnings, tracks, scents and threats, and nearly in my right
mind, I approached her territory to the entrance of her dwelling,
then returned— for what was written over the threshold
was a notice saying the time for my death had not come,
a command, really, though when I should return wasn't told.
So, I'm here still, save your verses for my later tomb,
don't let your heart turn brittle as mine has from her cold—
maybe you'll find another she's mistreated, whose time has come.

The Answer

Maybe the mist that seems not so much to cover
but reveal a grove of tender cypress as if it were glowing
is the way to describe her smile, and a bird calling
from that grove would be her love, and the wonder
would be the way my prayer seemed to blossom like a whisper
across my own face, and how I understood that living
in Paradise might be possible if that vision of her could cling
to my soul like vines of the morning glory— and flower.
The clear and certain pictures of angels we sometimes paint ,
the simple glance of a humble lover from the past, the call
of Love itself would seem like scorn compared to her
reply, for she looked to earth from where she stood among the saints
and seemed to answer through silence across Heaven's hall:
"Don't leave, dear faithful love, for we must last forever."

The Poetics of Love

I want to make her think the constellations have all wandered
into new formations, that the lake's moon is held a prisoner
each time she refuses to listen to these words, that the flowers
turn from her when she turns from me—a poetry not to be squandered
as in the past, not lost among the cries of the stars, unheard,
but carrying home, as the sparrow, in order to restore
its nest, carries one twig at a time, some new metaphor
that startles her soul into knowing what I have endured,
and into knowing what a prisoner she's been in her own heart,
and she will see this poem as some lost rose in the snow, fallen
inside her, or a relic some farmer unearths as he plows,
and then she'll know how her refusals only seem to chart
new lands and stars in this poem that finally transcends
all fears of me, and some new, some sacred love allow.

The Quandary

If this isn't love, then her heart's dealing from the bottom of the deck.
If this isn't love, then I've been given the wrong role in the wrong play.
If it is good, why does the sky seem to crack above me today?
If it is evil, why is my heart on the gallows, my soul on the rack?
If I burn by my own will, what heresy cast me into the fires?
If it wasn't my will, what good can any prayer accomplish?
Fate, choice, heart, soul, game, role or fanciful wish,
how does she have this power over me if I don't consent or conspire?
If I do consent—shut up, that's what I should do. I'm tumbling through some
emotional space like a new meteor, aimless, the proverbial
ship on a storm-tossed sea, smarter than some, dumber than others,
so I can't really tally the ledger on what's best for me or her
except to know I am poor without her, rich in memory, and begin to feel
death come each dawn, and most alive when my heart turns stone.

The Betrayal

So she duped me, placed me here on this target range,
left me like snow in the sun, like wax in fire,
like a cloud driven by a storm, an animal caught in a mire.
My voice stumbles after you like a cripple, and you arrange
to stay just out of hearing, until you turn, appearing to change,
appearing to offer a few words like coins to this beggar
who is your pilgrim, but you send wind, and sun, and fire—
you take aim and hold me in your sight like a stranger.
How could you do anything else? The idea of you is an arrow,
your face that sun, my desire that fire, your words that wind.
Love is death— and there's no end to the ways it can kill.
Your words are fallen angels, your sighs like the sea's undertows,
so that my faith burns, my desires drown, and every sign you send
pushes me like a refugee who has forgotten even the name for will.

Love's Contraries

Peace— I can't find it, but I'm not about to wage any war—
I fear the air that fills my words with hope, I burn in their ice,
I rise like smoke and grasp at a sky wrinkled with stars,
but the cosmos is a collapsed lung — there's nothing left to embrace.
Love is the senile jailer who neither opens nor locks the door,
who can't think of a way to torture me, or a way to cut the noose,
doesn't send assassins or come himself, but doesn't cut the bars,—
maybe he wants me displayed at market like a wild-eyed fish on ice.
I see with a stone for an eye and shout with a voice full of chaff,
I want to leap from a roof, yet Love coaxes me from his cliffs—
I hate what I've become, but love you dearly, like nobody else.
I live on pain instead of bread, and use my tears to laugh,
I despise, with equal opportunity, both death and life—
all because of you my dear, I enter this heaven, this hell.

Loyalty

Love, who lives and rules inside each hidden thought, each want,
who holds court over my conquered heart's coldest, dampest chambers,
sometimes parades out onto my own forehead in full armor,
sets up his camp, lights his signal fires, and plants his pennant.
Yet Conscience, who teaches us all to Love and suffer hurt with patience,
who wishes to douse Hope's embers, to rein in my great desire
with Reason's stiff rider, to guide my life by the hesitant star
of Shame, calls out the guard whenever she isn't given her proper reverence.
That's when Love retreats into the thickets of my heart,
when he surrenders even his ability to plan, to wish, to dream,
leaving his army confused upon the field, and trembles like a deer
caught in the hunter's sight, glancing wildly towards the fatal shot.
What can I do except stay, while, from his side, the hours drain?
He dies well who dies loving beyond love's hurt or fear.

The Turns

This humble creature, this heart of a tiger or bear,
who comes to me in the shape of a human angel,
turns me from hope to fear on the wobbly wheel
of her universe so that nothing is ever clear.
If she doesn't either stop me like some officer
or free me to tumble down some path, ravine or well,
I'll take the poison, the gun, the pills, or strangle
my own heart with bitterness until, somehow, it's over.
I can't bear any longer these sudden changes— my heart
gives out at her every word, or else it freezes, burns,
turns pale, tries to find its way back to the start.
Maybe I can flee into myself, invent a heart
that cannot feel, so cannot die, that cannot turn
away, cannot, out of jealousy, tear itself apart.

The Ruins

When I look out over eternal Rome pocked with ruins,
I begin to wince at my own crumbling past—
I cry out— "Get up, fool, slackard—cast
some sort of shadow—what in God's name are you doing?"
But then there's another thought that lines up for jousting
with this idea like a clumsy knight, and says: "Why run so fast—
Time follows your heavy tracks like a highwayman, and the last
chance you'll get to see your love is almost disappearing
into his ragged pocket." I understand it all then,
my insides frost over, I halt, like a messenger who hears
some news that twists his heart all of a sudden.
One idea returns at a gallop, another flees for fear,
changing places—I myself don't judge— the bet's even
money, bad odds in love, but it's been like this, this crazy love, forever.

Belief

Love and I, we stand apart, amazed, and full of wonder,
as anyone who has seen some incredible vision—
for we have gazed upon her, seen in her speech, her laughter,
that she resembles only herself, needs no simile or comparison;
and yet to talk of her—I see her brow, the falcon's
wing against the sky, her eyes that flicker
like a soul on a table that we mistake in our turns
for a candle, that brings a noble grace to this poor lover.
What a miracle to see her sit like a single lily that flowers—
—no, that seems to fill a field, or see her lean against a tree
as if she held it and the sky for all our hopes to breathe.
And what a privilege, now that spring is nearly here,
to see her walk out among her dreams, and then to see
her dreams growing with our love, all we need to believe.

The Waking

Now that the earth, sky and wind settle into night's still pool,
now that Sleep tightens its reins on every dream and scans
the stars that whisper as they slip below the fading horizon,
now that the sea freezes its waves and makes the tides stall,
I wake within a thought whose fire chars all dreams, all
hopes, a cold fire, a sweet pain, for Love has won
and lost, battled and sued for peace, posted bond
and released me to sleep only to wake again, a smoldering coal.
From Love's clear fountain I can drink both life and death,
can drink a sweet desire or choke on its acrid poison:
the touch of my Love's single helping hand can stab or heal.
It never ends, a waterfall that lives by falling to its death.
A thousand times a day I rise to die within this prison.
Each day I feel death's life, and die to feel.

Morning Song

I think it is her step that brushes the dew from the grass,
a step like some sort of goddess, maybe Diana opening
flowers, opening the morning sky, her presence reviving
the glow that slept all night in the lake like the moonlight's mast.
Love is what entangles the heart, breaks the soul like glass,
follows her step like some hunter— it's not her he's stalking
but whoever sees her, whoever opens his eyes to this morning,
to this light that falls like rain turning other desires to ash.
It's her walking that shows us where to go, her words
that tell us what to say, her wayward glance that tells us
what to watch, her gestures that tell us where to touch.
It's these four things that make a myth of every dusk—
I think I have become some sort of modern Tantalus,
I think I have become lost in the sun like a nightbird.

The Cave

If I had stayed to strike the match ends of stars in poetry's cave
instead of trying to break the worst dark night over my knees,
you might have had your poet now, someone who'd weave
a blanket against the cold, who'd bury every grave inside a grave.
If I had stayed to echo each fist of smoke, to work the soul's lathe
and shape a world you already knew by rote, to breathe each ready breeze,
I'd never know to cut the twisted vines from your heart's withered trees,
to spread my wings above your fire, or pull the dagger from the Milky Way.
Listen, the world beside this one cares little for us. It's an argument of stars.
Some say these crippled words are the smoke that abandons us for sky.
Don't listen. Even if it's only a light across the marsh, it can tell us we're alive.
I'll reap whatever I need from thistles and thorns with this broken scythe
of a poem, and, one hand filled with dirt, the other clearing away false stars,
I'll sow a world in every smile of yours that lately had become a scar.

The Pause

Let's stop time, Love, to see what those clouds yearn
to be, to listen to that butterfly stir the air around us,
to hear, at dusk, the stars begin like crickets, tremulous,
or feel their light begin to ripple in the lowest ferns;
let's see how skillfully the night covers this field of moons,
the way your own look has passed the sentries of my heart—
let's add some message twig to this nest we'd set so far apart
we only spoke with words that waited all winter in their cocoons.
Not long ago my sky was full of razors, the wind
had pried the roots of hope— now every mountain dreams
to hold your step, every tree has begged to give you shade—
the whole sky wakes like struck flint, a hawk reinvents the wind,
the huge valleys of the flower open their unimaginable scenes,
every clock drowns in your eyes for this world that will not fade.

The Collapse

It's not because this body has collapsed like a dying star
that I must give up loving anyone, give up these trees that neither
heat nor frost had harmed, let bushels of hope rot, abandon my flowers,
but because she has left me, lost faith in me, because she's shunned
all we had and were. You'll see camels where the ocean
was, you'll see stars fallen like broken glass on the sidewalks,
you'll see birds stuck to the sky's tar, before the safe box
of my heart spills open the love and hate for her that's held within.
It will never end: those beetles used to clean the coroner's corpses
will finish with me, Despair like some neighborhood butcher
will wrap up my flesh at $2 a pound, before I ever stop.
Planets will dissolve, wars stop, Death himself be stopped
and arrested at some remote checkpoint before her image ever collapses.
Even tomorrow's sun, lost on the other side of the planet, has no future.

The Hunt

Those sweet hills where I left the self that I will be and always was,
that self I left encased in a waterfall which hangs like a frozen sleeve,
those hills whose memory hunts me as I hunt it, where I grieve
and delight in this burden that has become my life's cause—
those hills, that maze, where I find myself in eternity's pause,
where every path I cross is the same path, where to love is to believe
that the beautiful yoke of these hills and self can never be relieved,
those sweet hills— no matter how far I go the closer to them I draw.
I'm like one of those gutted deer hunted in myth or in reality,
it's all the same now, that the hunter drags from the forest in a cart,
that froze momentarily on a ridge, heard the hunter's aim, unable to flee,
and crashed wildly then through the underbrush of the heart,
arrow hanging from its side, but almost thankful for the pure bounty
it offers, tired with its pain, tired of living so long and so far apart.

The Trailhead

Desire puts her spur to me, Love guides me
with her scouts, blazes the trail that Pleasure marks
falsely, that Habit, leaning over my torn maps, carries me
through. Meanwhile, Hope, like some backwoodsman, stalks
my heart. Why don't I ever see how these companions mock
my life? Why do I follow this gang with their camouflage, their masks
and deceptions, their tripwires, their ambushes, their planted tracks
leading to mossy cliffs, to white water rivers where every dream is blocked?
I remember Virtue reading by a quiet light, Honor guarding Desire's
broken door, Beauty opening herself in some mountain meadow
for the world to see —these were once my guides, my only signs.
How did I first enter this labyrinth, and why? What hour
cast its long shadow towards this moment that my heart can't let go,
my mind can't track, my eyes can't stop following, resigned.

❧ The Kiss

The way a snail dreams it might cling to a difficult sky like a future,
I dream to touch this nature of a queen, this intellect of an angel,
this soul that stalks me with its lynx's eyes that see through walls,
through mountains with their huts giving refuge, at their peaks, to the pure
words Love, exhausted from its climb, hums—Love, whose music is a finger
that traces a song lightly across my lips, or who, among some festival's
hundred random notes is by herself the gathering sonata that calls
the constellations into being, and who plays the world's cello like a cure.
No wonder the sunlight seems to root itself each morning in her soul.
No wonder, then, that this dawn has fractured the night, that some rival
claims her kiss. No wonder that my lungs have seemed to fill with owls
searching for prey in the darkened woods of my own heart, that my thoughts
leave this pitiful trail of words leaking from under the mind's shell,
praising her beauty, her keyboard soul, imprisoned though never caught.

Her Soul

Her soul, that is the sole reason the quietest winds sew
their distant signals into trees, and her words, that blossom
on those branches as the light, like a cat, scrambles down—
they turn other souls into explorers abandoned on Love's ice floes
in search of her— but she's like some magical or legendary rose
hidden in an alpine crevice even the best climbers abandon.
My own soul is like the shadow of an extinct bird, and my own
wish is to leave this earth before I know how little of her I'll know.
It rains inside my dreams of her. I fear these nightmares—
a rib of clouds picked at by flocks of marauding crows,
relics of feeling strewn like broken pottery on a desert floor.
Don't let destiny, breathing down my neck, win its dare.
Don't let her know how this craft hides whatever it shows.
You'd have to graft two worlds together to find a soul so rare.

The New Style

You might think this new style—studded with metaphors,
woven with stars and invisible planets, with snow covered
mountains, with flowers, with sudden streams, almost unheard,
the hunter stumbles across, with the shy fox, the whistle of the deer—
makes my love too unreal, but it would take finer, deeper,
more elaborate figures than I know, more than these thatched words,
these sentences unable to stop at a meaning that's not blurred
by this foggy heart, this blind soul, that can see no better
than the poorest poets, yet aspires in its naïve pride
to rival Cicero, Virgil, Homer, Petrarch, Sappho, Catullus,
to invent new worlds from what hints my love leaves in my heart,
to transform the pitiful world I find like the poet Ovid,
because the world she lives in lies far beyond us—
the most exotic galaxy, nebula, comet, is only a place to start.

The Fear

I fear the sky will barely look at me when I remember
the day I left her, and that the heart I left will be a silence
eaten by owls for what I did, that the stars will be a fence
keeping my soul trapped here like a hunted animal forever.
The moon saddened by its own eclipse— that's how I see her.
And yet she is still a bright planet against the dense
wall of stars, a flower in my desert, and she sees no sense
in fearing what I fear, no sadness, no cold, no fever.
She has taken off the seas, the wind, the hills, the trees,
all similes that try to hold her, and leaves no prayer
to call her back. I fear that what she takes off most is my world.
At least that is my nightmare, my despair, sad augury—
never to see her again, the sky erased, the stars at war,
the seas frozen. The terrible banners of hell begin to unfurl.

The Solitary

I have always trailed that solitary life whose difficult tracks
always seemed to disappear into streams and cliffs, meadows
and thickets, and have sought to escape the city's shadows—
Envy's disguises and traps, Pride's politic attacks,
the sneering envoys of Jealousy who turn the stars to pine black.
And if I couldn't find a home among these Tuscan hills to console
myself by their peace, perhaps in those hills where my Love stole
away, where every forest sound, every smell, every taste calls me back.
But the trail seems too often lost. Solitude always dissolves
into a crowd and I find myself again at my heart's trailhead
where my own past seems caught in mud holes and brambles—
though I once loved there, loved simply, alone, resolved
to remember how she, reading the few words I said
without speaking, knew my single heart, and these fitful symbols.

Her Death

That face that took the faces from the clocks! that glance
that took away the need for sight, that carefree manner
that took the chains from this lonely prison-world forever,
that speech which humbled savage minds, which put the lance
in the hands of cowards—and that endless smile which by chance
found its way like a dart through brambles to my bower,
that now is my own death too, and that soul, deserving an empire
of Love if she had not descended among us, putting us in a trance—
it is you—for you I must burn, for you I draw my only breath,
for I—I have been only yours, and as you leave me, more
than with the deepest wound, the most dread disease, I die too.
Hope once sat awake with me each evening, Desire's breath
held me in my bed, and I felt the very end of all pleasure,
but now the wind, the dark, steal off with words I meant for you.

The Surrender

My life is a desperate refugee that Time's border guards can't stop,
that Death and his squads of hired hands pursue with forced marches —
you think I exaggerate?— even the Present and Past sign treaties, drop
their rivalry, enlist the Future which begins to dig its trenches
around every crouching Memory and Anticipation which want to lynch
this hour and every following one with their grief, so that everything is lost
to truth, and only my Faith, its tattered shirt, shouts alarms at the cost
of falling upon my sword like some bookish hero without a flinch.
What Love comes straggling back? Not one sweet thing, never,
to this embattled heart. Counterattack? Escape to love's outpost?
Forget it. The winds are gathering like gunboats in the harbor.
My one chance for love's been put in irons, made a common prisoner.
My pilot's exhausted, shell-shocked, like his shattered sails and mast.
And now, even the allied campfires we watched from these walls expire.

The Solution

What are you doing, Soul, what are you even thinking?
What's the word for a life the moment it is over?
Inconsolable soul, putting hope in stars with no owners,
why do you still set the fires in which your dream is burning?
Your smooth words and seductive looks are really describing
the cry of the snow as it touches the earth, the fissures
of the moon that are your scars, the whole sky in tatters,
the laments the nightingale spends the whole day gathering.
Your life's been a road of wrong rhymes and songs, the shadow
of your tears falls across flowers, and even your dawn
will droop on its stem, even your river will sleep in its bones.
It's the tracks of birds washed out on the sky that you need to follow,
it's the nest's last twig that will give you your consoling song,
the shadows buried beneath mountains that will point you home.

The Loss of Breath

I've breathed everything I have into these difficult hills
that overlook the flood plain where she was born,
that woman who held my heart in her hand with delicate skill,
who held that heart budding or bearing fruit, who has gone,
maybe forever, so that now even breathing takes too much will,
so that even seeing is something I fear to do, because the stars warn
against what I'm thinking, and the moon itself refuses, still,
to reveal the cliffs and rivers, the towers and windows of scorn.
There's not a shrub or stone in these hills, not a leaf
left on these tress, not a flower left from what I gave her,
not a single blade of grass that does not mean her name,
not a spring, not a cabin, no fire, not even the smoke of belief
to hope she might return, not even the wildest beast, no tiger
in the shadows that would make this wild grief seem more tame.

Inspiration

If I thought anyone would touch the skin of these lines, hold dear
her voice that falls like an autumn mist through these rhymes,
I would have started writing when my heart scattered that first time
into the far corners of impossible words, and written more, and better.
Now she's gone, and midnight owls sweep through the forest like fear.
There are no high motives, no lofty thoughts left to climb.
There's no way now I can ever file down these rough rhymes
or forge the poor ore of my story in a manner that's sweet and clear.
All I ever wanted was to climb some ladder into her heart,
and when music and art fell, I tried to climb these scattered rhymes
to keep my mind from stumbling — not to rise to any fame.
The only good these poems have done is to show how far apart
we are, and if I were willing to write for fame, it would be love's crime,
for now I hear her call from above, in a voice that puts mine to shame.

The Valley

So this is the valley carved by words that drowned
trying to reach you, the river they damned up like logs,
the forest with its animals wandering through ground fog,
the fish trapped in streams like dreams the night ploughed
under. This is the valley where the air wipes the brow
of morning, wiping off my tears the way a flogged
man is helped by his torturer, or some hunting dog,
sensing his master's prey, never suspects Death's shroud
that covers the burrow he enters. I see you in these forms,
but never myself, for I have become a kind of inn
of fossilized love, some remote inn of infinite sadness.
It is from here I used to see you, used to pursue the storm
clouds of my heart before you rose above their wind,
rose, a pure spirit, discarding these images of madness.

The Debt

I turn to aim at those years rising like pheasants
from the brush to scatter my thoughts, those years
that cascade down ravines until they doused the fire
that burnt so cold I was frozen and scalded in an instant;
when I see Love break its vows and issue the warrant
that sends me to a church which becomes a sepulcher,
or that sells my soul like a slave, or, like some blind astronomer,
redraws the universe by some invisible theory or fear, I'm frantic:
my whole world suddenly stands naked among the stars,
so much so that I envy the worst collision of planets
as nothing compared to what I feel, this emptiness, this suffering—
Oh lost star, oh Fortune, oh Fate, oh Despair never lurking far
away, oh day whose sweet richness turns quickly into debt,
to what a low place you've sent me where the only pleasure is dying.

The Plea

Dear Soul, now that you have untied breath's subtle knot
that fastened your voice to earth, which now becomes a kind of hell,
think of the way, in the dark caves of my own heart, I dwell
like some homeless dream gazing into the pond of what it forgot,
and think of the way your bright cold moon hid my star's dim lot,
the way inside each husk of my hope some blight of despair held
every kernel of a future for ransom, the way these words, in stealth,
have struggled for days towards wherever you are, or are not.
Look to these mountains and you'll see me blindly wandering
like the survivor of some flood or fire —or —some solitary
hound poking under the roots of memory, Love's scavenger—
but no, don't look at that place under the moon's wide ring,
where we first met—pretend it never existed—or better, bury
whatever it was about me that displeased you then, or now, forever.

Love's Inferno

I felt like Dante's bumbling Pilgrim, lost in the dark
woods, off the trail, what he called the straight way,
a metaphysical path to heaven, wandering under a gray
sun, turned back by the prison walls of my love's heart,
so that now I've become some hunted beast in a stark
desert of broken lines and rhymes, and can't even pray
to be saved. I drag my own heart behind me, easy prey
to her hunter words following their syllable's terrifying bark.
So I'm condemned to wander here through Love's Purgatory,
looking for some trace of her, anything she's left behind.
I'm sick, yes, and Memory's leeches have done their best.
Everywhere she's been are things I can hardly bear to see,
always pointing away from Dante's hellish lakes of burning sand,
towards a place I'll never see no matter how much I confess.

The Birds

I thought my wings were words wide as a heron's to soar
on Love's graceful currents, to sing in its clear sky
above the tangle of base desires from which only
Death could free me, or only Love itself restore
my soul. I found myself like a branch some storm tore,
sagging with the weight of crows, or a meadow gone dry
as a desert, or a bird whose broken wing no longer flies
beyond all reason, towards heaven and her who I adore.
There's no word or feather light enough or clever
enough, no style or metaphor strong enough, no love
pure enough, to compare with Nature itself
when it created her, this impossible, marvelous border,
or with Love who always followed her like an angelic dove—
except by some chance word that glimpses her in Love's spell.

The Loss of Myth

In a happier time I might say it's Zephyr, not this spring wind
that returns, scattering red flowers, fresh seed, and I'd name
his mythic entourage, the woven song of Procne, and not some kind
of simple bird, a turtle dove, say, but Philomela's plaintive refrain.
I might say it's Zephyr that clears the skies at winter's end,
clears the meadows, that it's Jove there, delighted to see Venus gain
some new young love, and not just the earth, the sky, the water brimmed
over with feeling, that it's Love which remakes the senses, the soul, the brain.
But for now, I have to say that any Zephyr only returns with winter's
heaviest song, a kind of sigh, a draft under the heart's door
which can't be opened, because my Love has carried its key to the stars,
a kind of myth itself, I know, the way birds, still, make their poor
laments to beautiful lovers below who seem to have drifted too far—
because I have become a desert now myself, a wild, a barren moor.

The Nightingale's Lament

That nightingale's song, that vine playfully climbing the sky
to strangle the light, that spreads over the countryside,
over each flower, each stream, each memory to hide,
with its sad beauty, all love and hope of love, won't fly
into some other night, but tints my soul with despair's dye
to remind me how foolishly I tried to serve at Love's side
as if she were immortal, as if the weeds of my own pride
would be enough to strangle death by my petty sighs.
How easy it is to believe in Love's hope, to believe
the moon would always be full, the planets never shift,
that any life would not rot at its very roots and leave.
And now I know why this bird's song plots to deceive
all lovers, why it warns us while Love sets us adrift,
why nothing that pleases us is a melody we can believe.

The Trial

Not the late shift stars sweeping the aisles of darkness,
not the sloops that seem to iron flat the distant harbor,
not the deer threading their delicate scent through the forest,
not all of History marching, raising glorious shouts like banners,
not the news he brought of you, tonight, love's best witness,
news that I expected all along, that no love ever lingers—
the way Diana's troop, spied upon, made such a fuss
they set the dogs on Acteon, tore him apart, blunderer
on their sacred plot— like him, my own heart's ambushed,
like his, buried beside my Love— so, no, nothing here
can save me now, not your eyes, not the memory of your smile,
nothing can save me from this mistake, my life, this disgust
for everything, this desire to be swept away like those dark stars
at dawn, whose life is a constant test, whose every breath is a trial.

The Legacy

Death's lightning etched my heart's tree against the night
as if the whole night sky were torn up by its deepest roots,
the branches scattered like fallen soldiers, the night
and tree ripped open and savaged like pillagers' loot—
and my love, which nested there, never taking flight,
seemed lost, too, while new muses, epic, came to dispute
her claims. Yet somewhere inside, hidden from the light
even of my soul, climbing like a vine from the blasted roots
of my heart, a new tree rises with something like a sigh,
a nest that holds my fragile prayers and passions,
yet seems outside as quiet as the leaves no one hears—
this prayer which flies towards heaven like a startled owl, flies
from its home, from this heart where love rooted a passion
that keeps calling out even if no one is there to hear.

Not Here

My days are deer leaping from sight before they are seen,
shadows spreading into night before the sun ever rises,
eyes that close without ever opening, masked disguises
with nothing behind them, bitter or sweet words that mean
anything but what they mean. The world's torn at its seams—
heart from mind, flesh from bone —and these eyes
that watched Love's body as it suddenly seemed to rise
like some saint towards heaven now only blaspheme
her memory, for she lies beyond the gauze of stars,
before and after any time I knew her, like some comet
whose life is mostly beyond our sight, whose solitary life
is life itself. And so as my own life seems lived from afar,
my hair turning, my body failing, I struggle within Time's net
to dream her soul beyond all time, beyond this veil of strife.

The Messengers

I'll send these words out like thieves to scour every inch and yard

of earth, break the stone padlock that hides my Love like stolen treasure,

these words from languages of star, planet, bird, mountain, river,

hoping she'll shine from heaven, though here she's the envy of night, hard

for me to accept; and so, dear Words, tell her I myself am tired

of living, of trying to steer my way through the waves that batter,

horribly, this ship of a poem, a life; and Images, show her I still gather

the scattered leaves of our lost love threatening to kindle a wildfire;

and you, Metaphors, tell her that I described that edge of a flower's petal

by what her soul inspires, that I described the depth of the Milky Way

by what her touch has meant— tell her I want everyone to read it here—

but tell her, finally, tired and crippled words, how you too are only mortal,

how you'll stumble on earth a while then, between two galaxies, sway

until you fall not down but upwards, weightless, to meet her.

To Death

Death, just because you have eclipsed the world with your shadow,
have created another ice age where Love shivers around cold fires,
where Grace lies naked and abandoned, where Beauty grows too tired
to lift its head, I shouldn't have to carry this glacier of guilt that grows
then shrinks again inside me. Courtesy is exiled. Honesty now tiptoes
through back rooms. Our whole world has been sunk in your cosmic mire.
And why?— because you have uprooted that one seedling of pure desire,
she who was a sun, who held within her the whole world like an embryo—
so that now the whole earth should turn into a tear that tumbles through
the universe since we are powerless to take her back, and so we hover
as fields without flowers, rings without gems, fires without light, parts
without the whole. No one, not the world, not you, Death, ever knew
her as I did, how each glance of hers was a shield that covered
me from harm, that now covers heaven with a grace beyond my art.

The Model

From the flowers she hovered over as delicately as a hummingbird,
from the wind that learned from her how to caress the hillside
leaves and grasses, from the stars that copied her in filling the sky,
from her own voice without which the brooks could never be heard,
from her own heart that is the source of everything that stirs,
from her glance that pulls stronger than the ocean's tides,
and from her soul that is a light which calls pilgrims to her side,
from her body that the best sculptures can't capture without error,
from these I have taken life. Now they must delight
whoever populates the sky, and his attendants must stumble
over each other to please her, while I am left down here
waiting for some long held echo of her from some mountain's height
to finally be released, and pray she can hear, from the crumpled
flowers and trees, the darkened stars, how I long to be with her.

The Spirit

It is only very rare that such a fragile Goddess, such a frail
Soul walks among us, not as a shadow, not merely as a wind
we never see but sense, no—alive among us, appearing at Hope's end,
or walking the Heart's bridge each night Loneliness would send a wail
out over the darkening water, or helping each dream, each sigh scale
the walls that surrounded it. We thought this Goddess could mend
the stars that seemed to shift at each loss, or even lend
her gauze-like voice to quiet the storm more truly than the nightingale.
Maybe there never was the pure Beauty we thought she became.
Maybe there never was an earth so perfect we only imagined heaven.
Or maybe the earth has hidden, out of jealousy, all that she revealed.
Whatever she was has gone as quietly as dew: the sky is not the same
for it is only sky, the stars are only lights that refuse to burn,
and words, these words, are only angry lies, or lies that heal.

The Mask

Each day spawns a thousand others like a milkweed
bursting, and each of these I follow faithfully, as if Love
were leading me from each one, or planting a seed
for a better life, without anguish, where I wouldn't have
to live inside this shell, able only to deceive
myself. Sometimes there is so much light and love
inside my heart it, too, seems to burst, scatter like seed,
shine like stars through a fog, through storm damaged groves.
Death is not what we fear as it crawls into the light
we try to make, though we can imagine the sun's final pain,
as we stalk its tracks across the sky's desert,
and it, in turn, stalks us, reveals you nearly out of sight,
blown like seed, a star flung too far to see, a grain
of regret that shadows for a moment, our serene faces, far apart.

The Confession

Why all those years, those words, falling through the holes
of my pockets like the money the heart's careless traitors
waste trying to bribe this or that love with some worn phrase
that means she was more than she could be, more than mortal.
Now I must repair this tattered, empty basket of a soul,
this quartz heart that killed a love or friend with every phrase,
this scattered self whose glossy center was a prism ablaze
with false light, false hope, false love, a soul that crawls,
so that, just as the rotting glacier melts into the tree line,
just as the nightingale tries to repair the sins of our days,
perhaps my end will be some lesson for all of you to follow.
Whatever remains, know this: I loved poorly, a strangling vine
was my own heart and soul, a flower buried in the heart's cave,
yet still I hope, desire, love, and search for light like the blind mole.

Epilogue

...I then seemed to see a woman; she must have been from an age and a splendor impossible to describe, and of a beauty no one could ever understand.... and didn't dare raise my eyes...but heard her speak: "...I pity your errors, and have descended from a distant place to bring you the help you sorely need. You have been looking down at the earth too long and with your eyes clouded over."

Petrarca, *Secretum*

Love's Myths

No, I won't write my soul   against the sky that way again.

No more astrologer of the heart to skin   no words to hollow with disdain.

It's hard to be always in the rain   no matter what sun you live under.

You can sigh your images, scold   Love's splintered syllables—and then?

Nothing. Above the tree line, the mountain   snow never complains.

The dawn arrives in a train.   Therefore, I awake like winter.

Look, these lines are made to blunder   from grief to granite like dice.

Follow or not, they are love's price.   I can't control Love's plots.

I don't mind when Love's caught   fingering your days, planning its heist—

it's the way Love's pride darkens our skies.

Love rules his empire by never loading, or aiming, or firing a shot.

Anyone who turns his road into a rut   let him turn back now.

Anyone who twists that road can sleep the night in desire's field.

Anyone who dares to refuse Love's toll, you can yield

your heart, your breath, your being, everything you know.

I trusted Peter, crucified upside down,   and my own world turned over.

Believe it, Love turns you into a martyr   except salvation watches like a jailer

as Hope climbs into its own sepulcher   or carries the bag of its desire like a slave.

Love's not some rustic country town   you walk into like some casual traveler—

you end like Phaeton falling to a river   after failing as the sun's private chauffeur.

"Already the blackbird crosses that river,"   a proverb meaning, 'be brave.'

Maybe it's all like Plato's cave: we have to stumble out sometime

and Phaeton's comic failure to climb   the universe doesn't mean I have to quit.

A rock against the waves doesn't fit   itself into an ocean's vision like cheap rhyme.

You can catch small birds by using a sticky substance from mistletoe called birdlime.

What's most painful? Love's proud disguise, the Heart's counterfeit

coins, the totally incoherent alphabet   of desire. Too often it happens

that some rejected lover loses the stars above him, takes to living under bridges,

holding up signs at the roadside for work. Your life, then, slumps, walks to the edge

of the planet as if it could fly off, or invents some fantastic mythological end.

There's this proverb: "Love whoever loves you,"   first carved on a neolithic heart
or, as with me, made into a sort of art   that hides at what cost it starts to fade.
Love that doesn't love is a flimsy charade,   a poem you trust faster than you write it,
something you wear like a sailor's tattoo.   And yet humble Love is a hermit, lives apa
and there is no road map, no sea chart   to find her—no star you can use to persuad
her to return by. Love's safe in its own stockade   and you can't tunnel under it,
only be its prisoner without actually being *in* it.   It's not like some lakeside resort.
Infinite hope is the worst sort of spy's report.   Love can kill. And the truth is, finall
it's never arrested by the heart's police, never really   brought before the soul's court.
Maybe what little I have left to give might please someone, there's no fort
I'm going to hide in, no battles to plan. I'll trust finally
in some god that pretends to treat equally   anyone, who promises any sort of shelt
no matter if you are the most desperate fugitive, armed with distrust, jealous
even of the way the moon seems to wax and wane along a regular course,
because for him everyone who loves, everyone who grieves, is the heart's beggar.

If you are reading this like some Sybil   scattering the future in a pile of leaves

you might not understand. Whoever weaves   a net might not catch the bird.

If you are too subtle with these words   you'll probably break your mind's neck.

The sun waits a moment at the crest of the hill   before slipping under night's eave.

A rigid law only creates unease.   How many times we think a precious word

means something, only to find it obscured   by the way jealousy covers like a cloak.

Maybe hidden beauty, hidden love, are checks   we cash later. I bless the key

that turned in my heart like a plea   from some desperate parishioner

alone in her pew, offering every prayer   she's learned to release her agony.

Now my own Love is displayed on the heart's marquee.

And the irony is, where I sorrowed so long, chained to Despair's pillar,

someone else is now a prisoner   and my own sorrow becomes more dear.

I thank Love, then, for her book of rare if confusing symbols

you have to live to read. Life's prison is made of fine wool.

Everything's a fable with nothing at stake, nothing to really fear.

Silence is an infinite, hollow prison   where words, musical and wise,
hover in the dampest corners like sighs   from previous lovers, bringing the soul
life, as a light through a keyhole   promises a universe of sun and stars.
The night along the shore seems to mourn   except the violet shining on the tide.
A wild dog sometimes spies   a way into the city, then, bold,
creates a sweet fear in every household   that's happy to break from their harbored
lives. Look, from two springs one river   might emerge that links two elements—
like Love and Jealousy, meant   to live in one house, which means Love dies,
stars turn dark, the owl flies   from its nest as a kind of experiment
to see what lies beyond the night, to fly over dawn's battlements.
We never know what tracks us, never know the lie
inside each truth. The whole sky   is a law written with clouds.
Every peace is a trunk that contains the costumes for another war,
and every War walks into town disguised as a Truce with hidden scars—
but scars tell everything. I'm covered in a cloak made of these very words.

For my past harms I cry moonlight   and laugh with a mouthful of stars.

Sometimes gossip hangs like pears, scarred   from frost or envy, rotten.

You can't worry about what's hidden   in clouds—deadly floods or fertile rain.

You have to live in a little cell where sight   is hindered by Time's walls and bars.

The years since I first loved have traveled so far   they seem to lead to hidden

galaxies. The best thing is to fend   off the future and, from a safe nest, to gain

some high view of what still remains   of Love's burnt-out forest.

Maybe I wasn't bold enough, stood last   in Love's bread line. Hear this:

there's not a mountain's wish   not a sea's desire that will outlast

my love for you—there!—I'll nail it like an epic hero throughout the forest.

I can already see the rumors lurking like those shoreline fish

that catch at your shadows, or the bat's hiss   caught in a farmer's snare.

But what can words do?—my heart moves like the light across the lake

poking first in one bay, then some far point, leaving emptiness in its wake.

Live or die, freeze or burn, what you don't have you look for anywhere.

For those interested, the poems use as their starting points Petrarch's originals according to the following:

The Apology	I	The Trailhead	CCXI
The Battle	II	The Sparrow	CCXXVI
Desire's Escape	VI	The Exile	CCXXXIV
The Pilgrim	XVI	The Kiss	CCXXXVIII
The Prodigal	XXVI	Her Soul	CCXLVI
The Dreams	XXXIX	The New Style	CCXLVII
Desire's Departure	XLVII	The Fear	CCXLIX
To His Words	XLIX	The Solitary	CCLIX
The Prison	LVI	Her Death	CCLXVII
The Prayer	LXI	The Surrender	CCLXXII
The Promises	LXXVI	The Solution	CCLXXIII
The Declarations	LXXXV	The Loss of Breath	CCLXXXVIII
The Poet's Death	XCII	Inspiration	CCXCIII
The Window	C	The Debt	CCXCVIII
The Actor	CII	The Valley	CCCI
Love's Apology	CXII	The Plea	CCCV
The Rumor	CXX	Love's Inferno	CCCVI
The Answer	CXXIII	The Birds	CCCVII
The Poetics of Love	CXXXI	The Loss of Myth	CCCX
The Quandary	CXXXII	The Nightingale's	
The Betrayal	CXXXIII	Lament	CCCXI
Love's Contraries	CXXXIV	The Trial	CCCXII
Loyalty	CXL	The Legacy	CCCXVIII
The Turns	CLII	Not Here	CCCXIX
The Ruins	CLVIII	The Messengers	CCCXXXIII
Belief	CLX	To Death	CCCXXXVIII
The Waking	CLXIV	The Model	CCCXLVIII
Morning Song	CLXV	The Spirit	CCCL
The Cave	CLXVI	The Mask	CCCLVII
The Path	CLXXVI	The Confession	CCCLXV
The Conspiracy	CLXXXIV		
The Pause	CXCII	Epilogue:	
The Collapse	CXCV	Love's Myths	CV
The Hunt	CCIX		